Ebbs and Flows and In-Betweens

Kristina Susak

"What is done in love is done well."

Vincent Van Gogh

To everyone who has ever believed in me,
supported me,
and loved me as I navigate the ebbs and flows.

I cannot thank you enough.

XO

This is a collection of poems I have written over the years.

There is no rhyme or reason, no theme or cohesiveness. Consider this to be a copy of my journal – the one I take on hikes and long drives and open before bed most nights.

They are a reflection of my thoughts, experiences, and relationships formed throughout my life. Some are good, and some not-so-good.

Welcome to my brain.

2 January 2019

How is it possible
to live simultaneously
with chills and on fire?

Warmth captivates me
from your ice-cold eyes
and I'm trapped
in your sweet embrace

I love
wholly love
this smile so flawed
but so flawless

All I ask
is that you
teach me
to love like you do

14 January 2019

My mistakes
only magnify Your grace and mercy
Thank You, Lord

25 January 2019

The winds blow
and echo through my head
chilled to the bone
lonely, but not alone

All I can think of
is you, of home
and how warm it is
inside the walls of your arms

The fireplace glows
behind the blues of your eyes
and I sit
in the company of your crooked smile

12 February 2019

I want happy
I want healing

I want a path to walk
and the steps to take

I want to follow the Light
and never look back

I want the weight of the world
off of my shoulders

I want to live without worry
I want to celebrate life

I want to choose others
without forgetting myself

Because I have needs and wants, too

I want to laugh
without fear of the future

I want to breathe deep
without anxiety withering me

I want You
and I want me close to You
I want us
I yearn for an "us" again, Lord

11 March 2019

Sparkling like the sun
I look deeper; I see you
For all that you are

And not just the things
that you want them all to see
but the dark parts, too

16 March 2019

Your smile speaks in rhythm
with my heartbeat
and home feels like
laying in your arms

24 March 2019

My heart races
and my chest aches –
the dull kind of ache that lingers
My mind is in a flurry
as if it's blizzarding in my head
My eyes are tired
but brain is moving 100 mph
or maybe backwards
into the mistakes and problems and things in
the box
under the bed in my brain
that my therapist says I don't address enough
and this is why
I wish there was an escape button
that I could press
but instead
I press a razor to my skin
"all better," I think
as if causing pain will fix
the pain I'm already feeling

25 March 2019

I could light a thousand candles
but they would never shine as bright
as your eyes do

I could ride a thousand roller coasters
and it wouldn't compare
to the butterflies I feel around you

I could sleep a thousand days away
but you will still —
you will *always* have my heart

8 April 2019

May your heart never grow weary
and your steps never falter
May your eyes be set upward, forward
on all that is ahead

That sinking feeling in your stomach
that tells you you can't
is a liar
and you are stronger
than the voice that tells you "no"

14 April 2019

I crave being in love
with being alive
again
like I crave a flat white
on a chilly South Dakota day
or your arms around me
when we're miles and miles apart
Oh,
how I long to be
in love with life
the way I was in love
with you

1 May 2019

Maybe
we belong together
like Adam and Eve
or coffee and cream

And we can't undo
the mess we've made
but we can learn
and grow
and start again

8 May 2019

Is it wrong
to love someone
for the way they make you feel
or is that what we're supposed to do?

Because
I love the way you make me feel
I love who I am around you
and I'm beginning to think
that maybe
I just love you

For who you are
and who you want to be
and all your flaws
and all the beauty
that you don't see

So thank you
for making me feel again

9 May 2019

I seek a way to not feel numb
I'd rather feel
anything at all

I lean over the edge
I hold the pills
I search for the razor

Nothing

22 May 2019

You make your presence known
when it's impossible not
to notice you in the first place
and you scream my name
but not so anyone else can hear
You sit in the corner
and I try not to walk over
but it's impossible, yet again,
not to be drawn to you
with your messy 7 am hair and
obnoxious laugh and
gentle eyes that make me feel
like my heart falls out of my chest
You trot out the front door
and I can't help but watch you go
expectant for the next time
when my heart will feel as eager
as it does when you walk through the door

24 May 2019

I walked the streets
of a crowded city
collecting red flags from each nice boy
with nice eyes and a nice smile
ignoring the flags
that I painted pink in my
rose-colored glasses

25 May 2019

I don't fear
the wrinkles that are inevitable
with every laugh or wince
or moment spent in the sun
and I don't regret
the stretch marks that tell a story
I never could
because they are evidence of life
and if you ask me –
a life well-lived
So don't fear
the beauty of aging
because it is beautiful
in a way you couldn't begin to imagine

26 May 2019

I can't quite
figure out
if the feeling in my chest
is from you
or the fear that comes
with thinking about you
A beautiful blend
of nervous excitement
       butterfly-filled anxiousness
that inhabits my heart and
works its way up
until I'm sitting
in a puddle of confusion
made up of my tears
that I'm still questioning as to
if they're good or bad

And *this* is how much you messed me up

28 May 2019

Show me how it feels
to be craved
as the sun wakes us up
and the moon tucks us in

Show me what passion
can do to a person
when it's in the right hands

My soul aches for you

30 May 2019

I hoped you wouldn't notice
that I couldn't help but smile
at the sight of yours
though we both know
that you did
every single time

So you kept smiling
and I just couldn't
help myself

5 June 2019

Sometimes
I feel everything at once
and other times
I feel absolutely nothing
no matter how hard I try

13 June 2019

The urge to
pierce my skin
on the forearm of my
left arm
is usually in the
back of my mind
while I lay awake
while I drive
or read
when I'm in the shower
And the thought of my
loved ones
usually stops me in my tracks
but sometimes
rarely
I can't help but think that the
urges have purpose
and maybe it's my self-doubt
speaking louder than
anything else
or maybe
there is beauty
overwhelming beauty
in the fragility of human life
and in the urges we face
and conquer
or succumb to
and in the way the mind runs wild
when it's questioning itself

26 June 2019

I give you attention
and affection
and all the love this heart can carry
and in return I receive
well, absolutely nothing

It's incredible to me
how someone like you
can take and take
without the *slightest* inkling
that I may need something
anything
in return

But
on the bright side
you've opened my eyes
to the heart I am fully capable of giving
someone
as well as the love
that I undoubtedly deserve

28 June 2019

When I look into
your squinted eyes
and yours back into mine
there isn't anything in the
whole world
that could bring me the same
joy or hope or
tummy fuzzies
than in that moment

And
without fail
I forget there is anyone else in the room

All dancing
and drinking
and all I can focus on
is your side smirk
You call me a tease
and we sip on our beer
and wonder why we didn't think
to try this
long before

7 July 2019

And like the sun
in a setting sky
you fade away
leaving me dark
and cold
and blind
but I know that someday
maybe not soon
but someday
the sun will rise
illuminating my soul
like you once did
and I won't have to be
so damn worried
about the dark

16 July 2019

You call me beautiful
You care for me
You've washed me white as snow
You've set me free

I stand in awe
of the God of peace
and the love You have
for someone like me

And all my days
here I'll stand
head high
spreading love like a wildfire

22 July 2019

If there's anything I've learned
in the span of this lifetime
it's that love
towards yourself and towards others
is enough

Love is enough

Love heals
and solves
and mends
and connects
and unites
each and every one of us

And
in truth
love conquers all
without fail
when it's genuine and pure
and selfless and filled with grace

So maybe the answers
to all the questions
we're continually asking ourselves
can be summed up
by one simple command

3 August 2019

I can't mess up God's salvation
no matter how hard I try
because, you see,
I could never earn it in the first place

By grace
through faith

9 August 2019

Our hands inch towards each other's
as we stare at the illuminated screen
and our eyes meet
finally
After waiting all night
your lips find mine
and I wish they'd never leave
but they do
for a moment
so I wait and hope
that they'd meet again

Spoiler:
they do

27 August 2019

I refuse to be your back up
your second place
when I have given you
a first-place trophy
since the moment our eyes locked

I'm not your back up
and you're no longer
my priority

3 September 2019

Haunted by the ghost
of who we were
and it kills me
to know that you could not care less
about me

16 September 2019

I'm crammed in between seat backs
and tray tables
and look out the finger-printed window
to see lights — red and blue and yellow
but it's mostly dark
and all I can think about is you
What it'll feel like
to hold you again
and kiss you
over and over and
over again
until it ends
like it always seems to do
and I send you on your way
But first
you kiss my forehead goodbye
and I look into your eyes
with my fingertips next to your sweet dimple
and I can't help but smile
knowing it won't be the last time
but
I don't want this time to end
I hold you a moment longer
then you drive off
in your 4-door Lexus
and I board another plane
only to be surrounded by people
who aren't you

18 September 2019

The mountains are painted purple
and the sun
and the moon
still share the same sky
And all I want
is to share the same city
the same bed
with you, my love

19 September 2019

I'm high
and so are the stars
that are the same above me
as they are you
and I wish
that you'd come home to me

23 September 2019

You've created a garden
of joyfulness in my head
watering me daily
and giving me sunlight
and I can't help but wonder
if the changing seasons
the uncertainty of tomorrow
will cause you to forget about me

4 October 2019

It's not fair
that I can't take any of the pain
that you're feeling

And it's not fair
that I'm not the one
who's there to comfort you
and love on you
and pray over you

It's not fair
that you're struggling
and you're 1,400 miles away
and there's absolutely nothing
I can do about it
because you're there
and I'm here
and I'm in pain
thinking about the reality of the matter
which can't compare to the reality
you wake up to each morning

And I'm so sorry
that I'm not there

28 October 2019

I do what I don't want to
and don't what I do
yet continue to wonder
why there's an unspeakable
distance
between us — you and me
Lord, show me light
Let me see you in your
fullness again
I'm lost
and tired
and growing more and more scared
by the day

An ode to the Apostle Paul

30 October 2019

I lay in bed
yearning for you
and the mural of us
I have painted in my head

I pray I make you feel
the bright yellows
and deep reds
that you make me feel

And all I can do
is fall
rather, sink
into the melodic blues
that the distance draws

I absolutely adore you
and the masterpieces
you paint me daily

3 November 2019

What do I do
when all I want
is to give myself wholly
to you
but I promised myself
I would be whole
on my own
first?

4 November 2019

It's not fair
the love you make me feel
when you're not here to
squeeze me
or kiss me goodnight

And it's not fair
the pain I make myself feel
when there's nothing I can do
to make it any better

5 November 2019

There is an art
to making my heart
ache
and swell
simultaneously
but you
my darling
have mastered it

9 November 2019

How spectacular life is
when you're wholly in love
with someone
and wholly in love
with the life in front of you
and working day by day
to be wholly in love with yourself, too?

That's *magic*

12 November 2019

For from Him
and through Him
and to Him are
all things
and to Him
I will to run
into the embrace of a Father
whose love is for me
in all things
and through all things

A tribute to Romans 11:36

13 November 2019

Cover me in love
and hold me tight
Kiss my lips
Rock me goodnight

14 November 2019

I lay in bed
anticipating the days
the months and years
ahead of me
but pause in gratitude
for all that has happened already
to get me to where I am
at this very moment

Reflection

16 November 2019

Covered in your kisses
like I am in blankets
wishing this moment would never end
though I know it has to

But please don't leave me

17 November 2019

Above the clouds
that are delicately drawn below
and wondering
if you're looking up
thinking of me
like I am of you
And it's okay if you aren't
because when you're up here
you realize how small
and insignificant
life can be at times
which only makes me miss you
and love you
even more

20 November 2019

I often wonder
what makes your heart tick
and your head go blank
and the first thing you think of
when you wake up
because I desperately want it to be me

And I want you to wonder about me
when I'm not there to hold your hand in the car
or kiss you goodnight as you're half asleep
mostly because
you make my heart tick
my mind go blank

Oh, darling, you're all I think about

25 November 2019

I so wish
that I could fall into you
at the end of a long day
and look into your eyes
and tell you that you're my world
    my rock
    my love
And show you how it feels
to be truly
madly
deeply
in love

26 November 2019

Run your fingers through my hair
and kiss me gently

Look into my eyes
and tell me you love me

28 November 2019

At one moment I'm sitting
   surrounded by people
and the next I'm sobbing
   in an empty bathroom
and I can't seem to find
the trigger
The one that makes me
want to pull the one in my hand
while I stare down the barrel
with shaking hands
and sporadic breath
until it ends

It all ends
then there is peace

2 December 2019

I can't escape
the joy you bring me
and sometimes
I just want to be miserable

But I guess I can thank you
for allowing me to see the beauty
   the wonder
   the inspiration
that this world has to offer

So thank you
for opening my eyes
for loving me so tenderly
and so recklessly

9 December 2019

Teach me to see my value
to know I am beloved, loved
to rely on who You say I am
let me be wrapped in love
engulfed in grace
drowning in mercy

May I stop doubting my own heart
May I accept the kindness I am given
knowing I'd give it right back
in a second

10 December 2019

It's overwhelming
truly incredible
the amount of love
a single person can receive
in a single day

I am loved
I am valued
I am worthy of love
I am worthy
             period

11 December 2019

You let down your walls
and I came sprinting in
All I want to do
is build them back up
with both of us inside
protecting ourselves from
the ones who can't
and won't
understand
what this love is like
in the paradise we've built

17 December 2019

How much comfort I find
knowing that you and I
live under the same sun
and sleep under the same moon
even knowing we are
far too many miles
a p a r t

24 December 2019

I didn't think
that I'd ever find
a love like this —
one that wraps me in love
and showers me in kindness
and lights my fire each day
But how magnificent it is
to have found it
in a place
so unexpected

25 December 2019

I resent the fact
that being merely reminded of you
brings me to tears
And I mildly resent myself
for falling so deeply in love with you
But here I am
loving you anyway

27 December 2019

If only it was your soft lips
that wished me goodnight
instead of the stuffed bear
you got me
that could never remotely replicate
the feeling of being wrapped up in you

29 December 2019

My favorite thing about you
isn't your kind smile
or the dimples that outline it
and it's not the way I fit seamlessly in your
arms
and it's not the way I feel around you, either

It's the way you look at me
and tell me you love me
and make me feel like
nothing bad can happen
and the way I trust you
when you tell me that I'm all you need

30 December 2019

I feel at home
in your arms
There's a peace
I've never known
and a love
I now can't live without

2 January 2020

It's incredible
really
that we all use
different words
and stories
to describe the same single experience

Every poem
and book
and song –
each different

I'm in awe
of the fact
that we have a way
to portray how we feel
so individually –
uniquely crafted in each moment –
yet relatable to so many
and I think that's why
I fell in love with poetry

5 January 2020

I want a
photo on the dashboard
kind of love

7 January 2020

I miss you. And not in a dumb, I-just-want-a-hug kind of way. I miss you. In the way that makes my heart ache. My eyes tear up. I miss you in a way that makes my soul yearn for yours. To be wrapped in your love and drown in your eyes. I miss your presence. The joy. The car ride conversations. The airport squeezes and mouthed "I love you"s. I miss you. All of you. I'm wound up by the anticipation of being near you. And the promise of distance finding an end. I miss you. And I can't wait to see you.

12 January 2020

He is my muse
the magic that keeps me going
my everything

17 January 2020

You left just this morning
and a part of me feels
as though it's missing
like you robbed me of wholeness
and I know
I'll see you again soon
but it's never soon enough

27 January 2020

You're crazy to love me
but I'm endlessly grateful
that you do
because I am far more
than in love with you

29 January 2020

The pain of missing you
I wouldn't wish upon my worst enemy
but to love you
and be loved by you
is one of life's greatest blessings

6 February 2020

I hate
how honest I am
on paper

8 February 2020

I'm browsing through pictures
as I await landing
and I pause on the ones
that bring me unexplainable joy
where my smile couldn't be bigger
and my eyes are squeezed shut

Take me back
to the times with you,
dear friends,
when we were all in the same small town
where life was simple
and the drinks were cheap
and the company was too good

Please
take me back
I miss my people

18 February 2020

He told me I deserved flowers
and sent them to my home
and I felt overwhelmed
each time I saw them on my dresser
because it's nice to be loved
as both words *and* actions

24 February 2020

If you're not sure of anything else in this world
I hope you're sure of you and I

I hope you're sure that we can conquer the
world together

As long as we're *us*
nothing is impossible

3 March 2020

Occasionally
you forget to water me
and I shrivel up a bit
before you notice
But
to be fair
I am one
very needy houseplant

7 March 2020

Once I learned
that there are
many, many
things
that I cannot control
I was able to breathe
deeper
and sleep soundly
and be thankful
for the present
instead of worrying
about what is
in front of and behind me
and what peace,
comfort,
joy
I found in enjoying the *now*

12 March 2020

I am thankful every day
that we found each other
that God placed us together
that it's you and I in this life
that it's you and I
against the world

19 March 2020

Loving you is like
taking a breath
of fresh air

Absolutely effortless

24 March 2020

Send me to bed
after enough kisses
(I'll tell you when)
and never wake me up
from this dream

30 March 2020

I want to memorize
every curve on your body
every freckle
every scar and mark
I want to know you
more than anyone ever has
and ever will
and I want to love you
even more with each passing day

I love you today
and I promise
to love you more tomorrow
and more the next day
because that is what someone like you deserves
You give so much love
and I take so much each day
and I pray that my love
fills you
as yours does me

31 March 2020

Let's be still — I tell myself
Wine glass in hand
and I glance out the window
and I see a young girl
with bleach blonde hair
skipping down the street
and I reminisce

"Oh, how you've grown"
I tell myself
"Don't stop here"

1 April 2020

If I could tell every person in the world
the value
of *knowing* your worth
and *believing* you are worthy
I would have no words but those

4 April 2020

Like a sunflower
whose face is always pointed to
the sun
There you stand
heart
head
soul
pointed where the light is
and I strive
to be in the sun
like you are

6 April 2020

Sometimes
when things seem to be spiraling
and I can't find peace
I pause
and look at my wrist
and await the stillness
that allows my pulse to show
only faintly

I find comfort
even if it is merely because of the fact
that I am *alive*

There is life to be worth lived
and I am thankful
that I am here to do so

8 April 2020

I hate the fact
that I am forced to rely on
technology and fuzzy
phone screens and
poor connections
in order to see you
and love on you
and grow with you

9 April 2020

You say that you love me
and it's not that I doubt that
even in the slightest
It's that I've never known a love
to feel like this
so pure and honest and tender
so is it really possible for you
to feel that same love?

Is it possible for you
to see me
actually see me
flaws and all
and love me despite them?

10 April 2020

I find it truly magnificent
that the sun manages to rise
each and every morning
and the moon greets us each evening
without question
and the stars glisten and gleam in its company

And I find it magnificent
that I was given breath to face the day
enough air in my lungs to breathe with ease
and a sun that shines on me
and a moon that watches me dance
and cry
and sleep

I am understanding
more day by day
that this life
is absolutely
magnificent

11 April 2020

"I have never loved another human
as much as I love you"

12 April 2020

When you focus on the good
however simple it may be
the good overflows
despite the not-so-good

13 April 2020

I swear
my brain tries to ruin
every good thing
as if
it wants me to suffer
and I'm struggling
to keep fighting
the same battles
over
and
over
and
over

14 April 2020

Anything?
I ask

There is no way you mean that
I think

Anything
he says

15 April 2020

I struggle
to not compare myself
to every kind
and lovely
girl I see
until I remember
that I, too,
am kind and lovely
and worthy of good

16 April 2020

How I'd love to be
just *be*
with you again
holding hands on the couch
or walking around a city
we've never been to

I'd give anything
just to be held by you
and kiss your sweet lips

17 April 2020

My ideal day?

I'd love to wake up early enough to see the sunrise. I'd love to sit on the balcony, admiring the mountains, with a hot cup of coffee in my hand. I'd love to look next to me and see your grin, like, *this is really our life*. I'd love to talk about embarrassing stories and learn more as to why you're *you*. I'd love to take a car ride to the middle of nowhere, windows down, and blast our favorite songs. I'd love to have dinner on the coast and watch the sun set over the water. I'd love to tell you that I love you in this moment. I'd love to walk to a local ice cream shop and eat 'til our bellies hurt. I'd love to cuddle up in bed and fall asleep to some rom-com that we don't pay attention to. And I think, the part that makes it ideal, more than anything else, is having you there. *You* are my ideal day, every day.

21 April 2020

To love you better
than you've ever been loved –
I didn't know my life would be
consumed with loving you
but every day,
I'm thankful all over
for the chance to wake up
and love you again

22 April 2020

Being lost in the mountains
on an afternoon hike
with the storm clouds chasing me
feels natural
Being lost feels natural

23 April 2020

I'd say
I have mastered the art of
missing you
in between daydreams
and blank stares
and an empty bed
that's too cold without you

24 April 2020

I find it so much simpler
to climb the mountains
in my backyard
rather than the ones
in my head

26 April 2020

I'd love
to kiss you softly
and sweetly
and all over
until no part of you
was untouched
by my lips

27 April 2020

From the top of a mountain
the trees flow together like waves
and it reiterates the feeling
of being oceans away from you

28 April 2020

And in every crowded room
yours is the only face I see
and all I could ever want
is for you to see me, too

29 April 2020

The chances
of you and I
were slim to none
but we really ran with that chance

Let's never look back

30 April 2020

I love you more each day
and every yesterday
I didn't think it were possible

1 May 2020

If there is anything that I have learned
in my 23 trips around the sun
it's that

each and every one of us have a calling
that binds us together

to love
and be loved

2 May 2020

I'm going to hold peonies
and baby's breath
and stand between groupings
of all the people who love us
and we're going to make promises
and you're going to kiss me
and I'm going to love you
as long as I live

3 May 2020

I imagine you down on one knee
and I picture myself saying yes
and I can't help but fantasize over us
saying yes to each other every day
for the rest of our lives

4 May 2020

Smiles between kisses
are smiles in their purest form

5 May 2020

You tell me that I'm your sunshine
and that you're my little rain cloud
and I think it's quite poetic
because sometimes I seek sunshine
and joy and light
But other times
I love the sound of thunder
and cuddling up during a storm
and turning on a good playlist
and I don't think one is necessarily
worse than the other –
it's all about perspective

So today
I'm thankful for the sunshine
and the rain clouds
because neither would mean much
without the other

6 May 2020

The amount of love
you have for me
both comforts
and absolutely terrifies
me

7 May 2020

I'm beginning to think
that long distance
is just the accumulation
of missed hugs and kisses
and that the reunions
are never long enough
to make up for lost time

8 May 2020

We were sitting in my car
and we were high
and when you kissed me
it felt as though
I was floating through space and time
and I've never felt
so weightless
and so free
as I did in that moment
with you on a Friday afternoon

10 May 2020

Sometimes
not all of the time
but sometimes
I feel like I'm drowning
like the only solution is to end it
like I'll never be able to see the shore again
like it's all darkness from here

But I've found
that there are people
there are books and trails and songs
that bring back the sun
There are words that glue me together
and hugs that bring light back to my bones

And I've found that
regardless of what happens
they are right
it does get better
there is light
there is hope
there is joy
and it can be yours

11 May 2020

I'm absolutely
smitten
by you
and
the goofy smile
you give me
when you want something

12 May 2020

Anxiety is fiddling with your keys when you can't stand to be around people for another minute and it's crying as soon as you get to your car and it's texting them that you had a great time despite your near panic attack in the bathroom

Anxiety is not being able to fall asleep at night because of that one thing you said that could have potentially been misinterpreted

Anxiety is making up excuses to hang up the phone or not go out with friends

Anxiety is wondering why you're always feeling the way that you do and wondering when it'll stop, or if it ever will

Anxiety is constantly distracting yourself from the thoughts that are tapping on the glass cage of your brain
Anxiety is thinking
and thinking
and thinking
and not coming to a solution
because what if this happens
or what if this doesn't

Anxiety is a damn trap
and I'm sick of living in it

14 May 2020

I try so hard
to please you
and make you proud
but at some point
I'm going to need you to quit making me feel
like I'm nothing
like I'm not worth it

15 May 2020

Your love
stops time
and I wish
it'd never resume

16 May 2020

I washed my sheets
but they still smell of you
and falling asleep
without you actually here
is worse than I could have imagined

17 May 2020

I've been fairly anxious
as of recent
Not the kind that's crippling
by any means
but the anxiety that lingers
It's present at the thought
until I find a new distraction
and I dread
each time it re-surfaces

18 May 2020

I want to be crazy in love
with the adventures of life
and with the people
I'm surrounded by
regardless of all that society
tells me to fear and run from

19 May 2020

It worries me
that we
as a society
believe that being changed by others
is inherently a bad thing

I believe that I have been changed
piece by piece
and I think it's for the better
that I love stronger
and find joy in the every day
and hope a little deeper

It's all for the better
and I am eternally grateful
to the humans who shaped me
into a greater *me*

20 May 2020

I am an
indecisive perfectionist
and it's no wonder
the world seems so tough

22 May 2020

In the ebbs and flows
and the in-betweens
that undoubtedly accompany
there's a life to be lived
and light to be found
and almost too much joy to handle
and this is not
the end
to that journey

Thank you for reading my first collection of poems.

Thank you for loving me in this way.

Thank you for taking a chance on me.

More than anything, I pray that this book can show my struggles in darkness, but more importantly, my joy that followed in abundant light. You, too, **will** make it through.

XO
Kris